THE MANAGER'S MANAGER

STRATEGIES AND TACTICS FOR EFFECTIVE LEADERSHIP

AF529469

DAVID ALAN BINDER

Pharos Books

All rights reserved. No part of this publication may be reproduced, stored in a retrieval system, or transmitted, in any form, or by any means, electronic, mechanical, photocopying, recording or otherwise, without the prior permission of the publishers.

ISBN: .978-93-58042-61-0
eISBN: 978-93-58042-60-3
©Publisher
Publisher: Pharos Books (P) Ltd.
Plot No.-55, Main Mother Dairy Road
Pandav Nagar, East Delhi-110092
Phone: 011-40395855, +14049995474
WhatsApp: +91 8368220032
E-mail: sales@pharosbooks.in
Website: www.pharosbooks.in
First Edition: 2023

The Manager's Manager
David Alan Binder

Contents

Introduction

In today's fast-paced and competitive business world, good management is more important than ever. The success of any organization depends heavily on the skills and expertise of its managers, who are responsible for leading and guiding their teams towards achieving key business objectives. As a manager's manager, your role is critical in ensuring that your team is performing at its best, and that you are contributing to the overall success of the organization.

The role of a manager's manager is multifaceted and complex. In addition to managing your own team, you are also responsible for working closely with upper management to ensure that your team's goals align with the organization's strategic objectives. You must be able to balance the needs and expectations of both your direct reports and your superiors, while also navigating the many challenges that arise in any leadership role.

One of the most important aspects of being a successful manager's manager is building strong relationships with both your direct reports and upper management. This requires excellent communication skills, the ability to listen actively and empathetically, and a deep understanding of the needs and perspectives of all stakeholders. By building strong relationships with your team members, you can foster a culture of trust and collaboration, which is essential for achieving high levels of performance and productivity.

Likewise, building strong relationships with upper management is critical to your success as a manager's manager. You must be able to communicate effectively with executives and stakeholders, and understand their priorities and goals. By building trust and credibility with key decision-makers, you can ensure that your team's objectives are aligned with those of the organization as a whole, and that you are able to secure the necessary resources and support for your team to succeed.

In this book, we will explore a range of strategies and tactics for effective leadership as a manager's manager. From developing a clear management philosophy and vision, to building a high-performing team, to managing change and performance, to navigating office politics and managing stress, we will cover a wide range of topics that are essential for success in this critical leadership role. By the end of this book, you will have a deep understanding of the skills and expertise required to be a successful manager's manager, and be well-equipped to lead your team to new heights of performance and success.

Chapter 1

Why be a Manager's Manager

Simple! "Everybody manages something- by David Alan Binder

Be sure to Practice Golden-Rule 1 of Management in everything you do. Manage others the way you would like to be managed.

Being a Manager's Manager means other Managers recognize the characteristics of a great manager. Being a good manager is okay, but who wants to be just okay. Managers will look to you for insight, for solutions, a natural leader, and they will want to emulate you since you are able to get things done, enhance employee performance. You'll be cream at the top.

There is a nationwide shortage of good management. There are so many managers who avoided managing by putting out fires, handling the crisis of the day, week or month. Basically bluffing, cajoling, incentivizing, browbeating, belaboring, driving.

There is no doubt that effective management is crucial for the success of any organization, yet there is a nationwide shortage of good management. Many managers fall into the trap of avoiding true management responsibilities by focusing on short-term problem-solving and firefighting. These managers often lack the skills and knowledge necessary to lead their teams to long-term success.

Instead of developing and implementing strategic plans, these managers spend their time handling the crisis of the day, week, or month. They become experts at bluffing, cajoling, incentivizing, browbeating, belaboring, and driving their teams to accomplish short-term goals. While these tactics may achieve immediate results, they are not sustainable in the long run, and they can lead to burnout and disengagement among team members.

One of the primary reasons for this shortage of good management is a lack of investment in leadership development. Many organizations fail to provide their managers with the training and support they need to effectively manage their teams. As a result, managers are left to fend for themselves, and they often resort to reactive, short-term management tactics.

Another factor contributing to the shortage of good management is the misconception that management is simply about telling people what to do. In reality, effective management requires a wide range of skills, including communication, collaboration, problem-solving, and strategic thinking. Managers who lack these skills may struggle to lead their teams to success.

To address this shortage of good management, organizations must invest in leadership development programs that provide managers with the skills and knowledge they need to effectively manage their teams. This includes training in areas such as communication, collaboration, problem-solving, and strategic thinking. Additionally, organizations must create a culture that values and rewards effective management, and that holds managers accountable for their performance.

In conclusion, the shortage of good management is a significant problem that is hindering the success of many organizations. To address this issue, organizations must invest in leadership development programs and create a culture that values and rewards effective management. By doing so, they can build strong, sustainable teams that are capable of achieving long-term success.

Being a manager's manager can be a rewarding and fulfilling role for a number of reasons:

1. The opportunity to develop and support others: As a manager's manager, you have the opportunity to develop and support your team members in their professional growth and success. You can help them identify their strengths and weaknesses, provide coaching and feedback, and help them develop new skills and competencies.
2. Influence organizational success: As a manager's manager, you play a critical role in ensuring the success of your team and the organization as a whole. You are responsible for aligning your team's goals with the overall organizational strategy, and for helping your team to achieve its objectives.
3. Continuous learning and growth: Being a manager's manager requires continuous learning and growth, as you navigate complex workplace dynamics and new challenges. This can be both challenging and rewarding, as you develop new skills and competencies and become a more effective leader.
4. Building relationships: As a manager's manager, you have the opportunity to build relationships with key stakeholders in the organization, including upper management, peers, and other teams. This can help you to gain insights into the organization and its priorities, and to build a strong network of support.

Overall, being a manager's manager can be a fulfilling and rewarding role, as you have the opportunity to support and develop others, influence organizational success, and continue your own learning and growth.

Chapter 2

Developing a Management Philosophy

As a manager's manager, one of your key responsibilities is to develop a clear and effective management philosophy that will guide your decision-making and actions as a leader. Your management philosophy should reflect your values, beliefs, and approach to leadership, and should provide a framework for how you will manage and lead your team towards achieving key business objectives.

Defining your management philosophy

The first step in developing your management philosophy is to define your values and beliefs as a leader. What do you stand for? What are your guiding principles? Some key areas to consider include your approach to communication, collaboration, accountability, and performance management. By clarifying your values and beliefs, you can ensure that your management style is consistent and aligned with your overall goals and objectives.

Creating a vision for your team and organization

In addition to defining your management philosophy, it is also important to create a clear and compelling vision for your team and organization. Your vision should be aligned with the overall strategic objectives of the organization, and should provide a sense of direction and purpose for your team. It should also be inspiring and motivating, and should help to rally your team members around a common goal.

Communicating your philosophy to others

Finally, it is important to communicate your management philosophy and vision to your team and other stakeholders. This can involve creating a written document that outlines your philosophy and vision, as well as engaging in regular communication with your team members to ensure that they understand and are aligned with your goals and objectives. By communicating your philosophy effectively, you can build trust and credibility with your team, and ensure that everyone is working towards the same goals.

In conclusion, developing a clear and effective management philosophy is an essential first step in becoming a successful manager's manager. By defining your values and beliefs, creating a compelling vision, and communicating effectively with your team, you can create a culture of trust, collaboration, and accountability that is essential for achieving high levels of performance and productivity.

Chapter 3

Building a High-Performing Team

As a manager's manager, one of your most important responsibilities is to build and manage a high-performing team that is capable of achieving key business objectives. Building a high-performing team requires a combination of skills and strategies, including identifying and recruiting top talent, fostering a culture of collaboration and accountability, and providing ongoing training and development opportunities.

Identifying and recruiting top talent

The first step in building a high-performing team is to identify and recruit top talent. This involves understanding the key skills and expertise required for success in your industry and role, and actively seeking out individuals who possess those skills and attributes. You should also have a clear understanding of your team's strengths and weaknesses, and identify individuals who can help to address any gaps or areas of improvement.

Fostering a culture of collaboration and accountability

In addition to recruiting top talent, it is also important to foster a culture of collaboration and accountability within your team. This involves setting clear expectations and goals, and creating a sense of ownership and responsibility among team members. You should also encourage open communication and feedback, and create opportunities for team members to work together on projects and initiatives.

Providing ongoing training and development opportunities

Finally, it is important to provide ongoing training and development opportunities for your team members. This can involve providing access to training programs and resources, as well as offering mentorship and coaching to help team members develop their skills and expertise. By investing in your team members' professional development, you can not only improve their performance and productivity, but also create a culture of continuous learning and improvement.

In conclusion, building a high-performing team is a critical component of effective leadership as a manager's manager. By identifying and recruiting top talent, fostering a culture of collaboration and accountability, and providing ongoing training and development opportunities, you can create a team that is capable of achieving key business objectives and driving long-term success for your organization.

Chapter 4
Leading Change

As a manager's manager, you are often responsible for leading and managing change within your organization. This can involve anything from implementing new processes and procedures, to introducing new technologies or products, to responding to changes in the market or regulatory environment. Leading change requires a combination of skills and strategies, including identifying and responding to changing business environments, managing resistance to change, and communicating change effectively to all stakeholders.

Identifying and responding to changing business environments

The first step in leading change is to identify and respond to changing business environments. This involves monitoring trends and developments in your industry, as well as keeping a close eye on your organization's performance and competitive position. By staying attuned to these changes, you can identify opportunities and threats early on, and proactively develop strategies to respond to them.

Managing resistance to change

Another key challenge in leading change is managing resistance to change. Change can be difficult for many people, and it is common for team members to feel anxious or uncertain when faced with new processes, technologies, or initiatives. As a manager's manager, it is your responsibility to anticipate and address this resistance, and to work with your team to help them understand the rationale and benefits of the proposed changes.

Communicating change effectively to all stakeholders

Finally, it is important to communicate change effectively to all stakeholders. This involves developing a clear and compelling message that outlines the rationale and benefits of the proposed changes, as well as addressing any concerns or questions that stakeholders may have. You should also develop a comprehensive communication plan that includes regular updates and opportunities for feedback, and that engages stakeholders at all levels of the organization.

In conclusion, leading change is a critical component of effective leadership as a manager's manager. By identifying and responding to changing business environments, managing resistance to change, and communicating change effectively to all stakeholders, you can ensure that your organization is able to adapt and thrive in an ever-changing business environment.

Chapter 5
Managing Performance

Effective performance management is a critical component of any successful organization. It ensures that employees understand what is expected of them, how they are performing, and how they can improve. In this chapter, we will discuss several key strategies for managing performance, including setting clear goals and expectations, providing regular feedback and coaching, and addressing underperformers and difficult conversations.

Setting Clear Goals and Expectations

Setting clear goals and expectations for your team is the first step in managing performance. This involves defining the key objectives, targets, and deliverables that your team should achieve. When setting goals, it is essential to ensure they are SMART - specific, measurable, achievable, relevant, and time-bound. Clear objectives help employees understand what is expected of them and give them a sense of direction and purpose.

Providing Regular Feedback and Coaching

Providing regular feedback and coaching is another critical aspect of managing performance. Regular feedback helps employees understand how they are performing and what they need to do to improve. It is essential to provide both positive and constructive feedback, as well as guidance on how to improve. Coaching can help employees develop their skills and reach their full potential.

Dealing with Underperformers

Despite the best efforts, some employees may struggle to meet performance expectations. In such cases, it is essential to address the issue promptly and professionally. The first step is to identify the root cause of the problem. This may involve a lack of skills or knowledge, poor motivation, or inadequate resources. Once the issue is identified, it is important to work with the employee to develop an action plan to address the problem. It may also be necessary to provide additional support or training to help the employee improve.

Another part of dealing with issues is putting full responsibility and control with the person. Outline for the individual consequences for actions both positive and negative and let them know it is their choice not yours. Document everything, date, time, those present and what was said by both parties. Particularly use repeat back to ensure that the person understands you by reiterating what was said and meant to ensure complete understanding anc comprehension. This is extremely effective in dealing with employees or subordinates that may be operating with other goals, or counter to instructions or rules or guidelines.

Difficult Conversations

Managing performance often involves difficult conversations. These may include discussions about missed targets, poor performance, or disciplinary issues. It is important to approach these conversations with empathy and professionalism. It is crucial to be clear and direct about the issue, while also being respectful and considerate of the employee's feelings. It may be helpful to prepare for the conversation in advance and to have a plan for how to move forward.

In conclusion, managing performance is a critical aspect of effective leadership. Setting clear goals and expectations, providing regular feedback and coaching, addressing underperformers, and managing difficult conversations are all key strategies for managing performance effectively. By following these strategies, you can help your team achieve its goals, develop its skills, and reach its full potential.

Chapter 6

Building Relationships with Upper Management

As a manager's manager, building strong relationships with upper management is critical to your success. Effective communication, trust, and credibility are essential to ensure that your team's goals align with the organization's strategic objectives. In this chapter, we will discuss several key strategies for building relationships with upper management, including understanding their needs and priorities, communicating effectively with executives and stakeholders, and building trust and credibility with key decision-makers.

Understanding the Needs and Priorities of Upper Management

To build strong relationships with upper management, you must first understand their needs and priorities. This involves understanding the organization's goals, strategies, and objectives, as well as the challenges and opportunities that upper management faces. By understanding these factors, you can align your team's goals and objectives with the organization's strategic priorities.

Communicating Effectively with Executives and Stakeholders

Effective communication is critical when building relationships with upper management. It is important to communicate regularly and clearly with executives and stakeholders, keeping them informed of your team's progress, challenges, and successes. When communicating, it is essential to be concise, clear, and focused on the key messages. You should also be prepared to answer questions and provide additional information as needed.

Building Trust and Credibility with Key Decision-Makers

Building trust and credibility with key decision-makers is essential when building relationships with upper management. To do this, you must demonstrate your competence, integrity, and professionalism. You can do this by delivering high-quality work, meeting deadlines, and communicating effectively. You should also be proactive in identifying and addressing potential issues, demonstrating that you are proactive and solutions-focused.

Another key factor in building trust and credibility is to be transparent and honest in your communications. If you make a mistake, take responsibility for it and work to correct the issue. If you encounter challenges or obstacles, be upfront and communicate these to upper management. This approach shows that you are accountable and committed to delivering results.

In conclusion, building relationships with upper management is critical to your success as a manager. Understanding their needs and priorities, communicating effectively with executives and stakeholders, and building trust and credibility with key decision-makers are all essential strategies for building these relationships. By following these strategies, you can ensure that your team's goals align with the organization's strategic objectives and deliver results that contribute to the success of the organization.

Chapter 7
Managing Up

Managing up is a critical skill for managers who want to succeed in their roles. It involves managing both downwards to your team and upwards to your boss and upper management. In this chapter, we will discuss several key strategies for managing up, including understanding the importance of managing up, navigating office politics and power dynamics, and building a strong relationship with your boss.

Managing Both Directions

Effective management involves managing both upwards and downwards. Managing downwards involves leading and developing your team to achieve their goals, while managing upwards involves communicating with your boss and upper management to ensure that your team's goals align with the organization's objectives. Managing both directions is critical to your success As a manager's manager.

Understanding the Importance of Managing Up

Managing up is important because it helps you build strong relationships with your boss and upper management, and it ensures that your team's goals align with the organization's objectives. It also helps you navigate office politics and power dynamics, which can be challenging for new or inexperienced managers. By managing up effectively, you can demonstrate your value to the organization and position yourself for future career opportunities.

Navigating Office Politics and Power Dynamics

Office politics and power dynamics can be challenging to navigate, especially for new or inexperienced managers. To navigate these dynamics, it is essential to understand the power structure within your organization and the interests and motivations of key stakeholders. It is also important to build strong relationships with key decision-makers, communicate effectively, and demonstrate your value to the organization.

Building a Strong Relationship with Your Boss

Building a strong relationship with your boss is critical to managing up effectively. To do this, it is important to communicate regularly and effectively, keep your boss informed of your team's progress, and seek their feedback and guidance. You should also be proactive in identifying and addressing potential issues and opportunities, demonstrating that you are solutions-focused and committed to achieving the organization's goals.

Another key factor in building a strong relationship with your boss is to understand their working style and preferences. Some bosses may prefer regular updates and communication, while others may prefer a more hands-off approach. By understanding your boss's preferences and working style, you can adapt your communication and management approach to better meet their needs.

In conclusion, managing up is a critical skill for managers who want to succeed in their roles. Emphasizing managing both directions, understanding the importance of managing up, navigating office politics and power dynamics, and building a strong relationship with your boss are all essential strategies for managing up effectively. By following these strategies, you can build strong relationships with key decision-makers, align your team's goals with the organization's objectives, and position yourself for future career opportunities.

Chapter 8

Building Resilience and Managing Stress

As a manager, you face numerous challenges and setbacks on a regular basis. Building resilience and managing stress are critical skills that can help you navigate these challenges and maintain your well-being. In this chapter, we will discuss several key strategies for building resilience and managing stress, including developing resilience in the face of challenges and setbacks, managing stress and burnout, and prioritizing self-care and work-life balance.

Developing Resilience in the Face of Challenges and Setbacks

Resilience is the ability to bounce back from challenges and setbacks. It is an essential skill for managers, who must navigate constantly changing environments and handle difficult situations. To build resilience, it is important to focus on your strengths and develop a growth mindset. You should also seek out support and feedback from your colleagues and mentors, learn from your mistakes, and maintain a positive outlook.

Managing Stress and Burnout

Stress and burnout are common issues for managers, who often work long hours and face high-pressure situations. To manage stress and prevent burnout, it is important to practice self-care and prioritize your well-being. This may involve developing healthy habits, such as exercise, meditation, and healthy eating, and setting boundaries to maintain a healthy work-life balance. You should also be aware of the signs of burnout, such as fatigue, irritability, and a lack of motivation, and take steps to address these issues before they become more serious.

Prioritizing Self-Care and Work-Life Balance

Prioritizing self-care and work-life balance is essential for managing stress and maintaining your well-being. This may involve setting clear boundaries between work and personal time, prioritizing activities that bring you joy and fulfillment, and seeking out support from your colleagues and loved ones. It is also important to take regular breaks throughout the day, such as going for a walk or taking a few minutes to meditate, to help you manage stress and maintain your focus.

In conclusion, building resilience and managing stress are critical skills for managers who want to succeed in their roles. By developing resilience in the face of challenges and setbacks, managing stress and burnout, and prioritizing self-care and work-life balance, you can maintain your well-being and achieve your goals As a manager's manager. Remember, taking care of yourself is essential for achieving long-term success, both personally and professionally.

Chapter 9

Managers Require Training to be Effective

The success of any organization is largely dependent on its ability to effectively manage its human resources. The role of a manager is critical in ensuring that the organization's goals are met and that employees are motivated and engaged in their work. However, not all managers are equipped with the necessary skills to perform their duties effectively. In this chapter, we will discuss the prevalence, mistakes, and dangers of using, hiring, and promoting people without manager training.

Prevalence of Managers without Training

It is not uncommon for organizations to promote employees to managerial positions without providing them with any formal training. In fact, according to a survey conducted by the Society for Human Resource Management (SHRM), 43% of new managers receive no training. This is a concerning statistic, as it suggests that many managers are not equipped with the necessary skills to effectively lead their teams.

Proper vs. Improper

The lack of manager training can lead to a number of mistakes being made. For example, new managers may struggle to delegate tasks effectively, leading to overwork and burnout among their team members. They may also struggle to communicate expectations clearly, leading to confusion and frustration among their team. In addition, they may not be equipped to handle difficult conversations, such as performance reviews or disciplinary actions, which can lead to further problems down the line.

Warning

The dangers of using, hiring, and promoting people without manager training are numerous. Perhaps the most significant danger is that untrained managers can create a toxic work environment. When managers are not equipped with the necessary skills to lead their teams effectively, they may resort to micromanagement, passive-aggressive behavior, or other forms of inappropriate conduct. This can lead to low morale, high turnover, and even legal action in some cases.

In addition, untrained managers may struggle to identify and address performance issues. This can result in underperforming employees being allowed to continue in their roles, which can harm the organization's overall performance. Conversely, untrained managers may also fail to recognize and promote high-performing employees, which can lead to these employees becoming disengaged and seeking employment elsewhere.

Conclusion

In conclusion, the prevalence, mistakes, and dangers of using, hiring, and promoting people without manager training are significant. Organizations that fail to provide their managers with the necessary training and support may find themselves struggling to meet their goals, retain their top talent, and avoid legal and reputational damage. It is therefore essential that organizations invest in manager training programs to ensure that their managers are equipped with the skills they need to lead their teams effectively.

Chapter 10

Management Succession

Management succession planning is a process that helps organizations prepare for the eventual departure of key leaders and managers. This process involves identifying potential successors, developing their skills and capabilities, and creating a plan to ensure a smooth transition when the time comes. In this chapter, we will discuss the importance of management succession planning and how organizations can develop effective succession plans.

The Importance of Management Succession Planning

Management succession planning is important for several reasons. Firstly, it helps organizations maintain stability and continuity during times of change. When a key leader or manager leaves, the organization can experience significant disruptions to its operations and overall performance. However, by having a succession plan in place, the organization can ensure that there is a clear plan for transitioning responsibilities to a new leader or manager.

Secondly, management succession planning is essential for retaining top talent within an organization. When employees see that there is a clear path for advancement and development within the organization, they are more likely to stay and invest their time and energy into their work. Additionally, by developing the skills and capabilities of potential successors, organizations can create a talent pipeline that can support their long-term success.

Finally, management succession planning is important for ensuring that the organization is prepared for future challenges and opportunities. By developing a pool of talented leaders and managers, organizations can adapt to changing market conditions, technological advances, and other external factors that may impact their operations.

Developing Effective Management Succession Plans

Developing effective management succession plans involves several key steps. Firstly, organizations must identify the critical positions within the organization that require succession planning. These positions are typically those that have significant impact on the organization's overall performance and success.

Once these positions have been identified, organizations must assess their current talent pool to determine who has the potential to fill these positions in the future. This involves evaluating their skills, experience, and leadership potential.

Once potential successors have been identified, organizations must develop a plan to develop their skills and capabilities. This may involve providing training, mentoring, and other developmental opportunities to help these individuals grow into their roles.

Finally, organizations must create a plan for transitioning responsibilities to the new leader or manager. This plan should outline the steps that will be taken to ensure a smooth transition, including the transfer of knowledge and key responsibilities.

Conclusion

In conclusion, management succession planning is an essential process that helps organizations prepare for the eventual departure of key leaders and managers. By identifying potential successors, developing their skills and capabilities, and creating a plan for transition, organizations can maintain stability and continuity, retain top talent, and prepare for future challenges and opportunities. Effective management succession planning requires careful planning, evaluation, and development, but can ultimately help organizations ensure their long-term success.

Chapter 11

Effective Communication for Managers

Effective communication is a vital aspect of successful management. As a manager, your ability to communicate effectively with your team members, superiors, clients, and stakeholders can determine the success of your business. This chapter will explore the importance of communication in management, the different communication styles, how to develop effective communication skills, and the importance of active listening and feedback.

Importance of Communication in Management

Effective communication is essential in management for several reasons. Firstly, it helps in establishing and maintaining healthy relationships with team members, clients, and stakeholders. It promotes transparency, trust, and mutual understanding, which are critical components of successful business relationships. Secondly, communication helps in ensuring that everyone is on the same page, and that there is a shared understanding of goals, objectives, and expectations. Thirdly, it helps in facilitating effective decision-making, problem-solving, and conflict resolution.

Understanding Different Communication Styles

There are different communication styles that people use to express themselves. These styles are influenced by cultural backgrounds, personalities, and personal preferences. It is essential to understand these styles to communicate effectively with different people. Some people may be direct and to the point, while others may prefer a more indirect approach. Some may be more comfortable with verbal communication, while others may prefer written communication. It is important to be aware of these styles and adapt your communication accordingly to ensure effective communication.

Developing Effective Communication Skills

1. Effective communication skills are essential for successful management. The following are some tips to help you develop effective communication skills:
2. Be clear and concise: Use simple language to ensure that your message is understood.
3. Use the appropriate communication channel: Choose the appropriate communication channel depending on the nature of the message and the recipient.
4. Be mindful of your body language: Your body language can communicate more than your words. Be mindful of your tone of voice, facial expressions, and gestures.
5. Be a good listener: Listen actively and try to understand the other person's point of view.
6. Show empathy: Show empathy by acknowledging the other person's feelings and concerns.

Active Listening and Feedback

Active listening is an essential aspect of effective communication. It involves paying attention to the speaker, understanding their message, and responding appropriately. Active listening helps in building trust and rapport, promoting mutual understanding, and resolving conflicts.

Feedback is also an essential aspect of effective communication. Feedback provides an opportunity to assess performance, identify areas of improvement, and recognize achievements. Feedback should be specific, timely, and constructive to be effective.

In conclusion, effective communication is critical for successful management. Understanding different communication styles, developing effective communication skills, and practicing active listening and feedback can help in promoting healthy relationships, facilitating effective decision-making, and achieving business objectives.

Chapter 12

Managing Diversity and Inclusion

In today's diverse and globalized workplace, managing diversity and inclusion has become a critical issue for managers. Organizations that embrace diversity and inclusion are more likely to attract and retain top talent, increase employee engagement, and boost innovation and productivity. In this chapter, we will explore the importance of diversity and inclusion in the workplace and provide practical strategies for creating a diverse and inclusive team, fostering an inclusive culture, and addressing issues of discrimination and bias.

Understanding the Importance of Diversity and Inclusion in the Workplace

Diversity and inclusion are essential for creating a dynamic and high-performing workplace. In this section, we will explore the business case for diversity and inclusion, including how diversity and inclusion can enhance creativity, innovation, and problem-solving. We will also discuss the legal and ethical imperatives of diversity and inclusion.

Creating a Diverse and Inclusive Team

Creating a diverse and inclusive team requires more than just hiring employees from different backgrounds. In this section, we will provide practical strategies for recruiting, hiring, and retaining a diverse team. We will also discuss the importance of creating an inclusive workplace culture that values different perspectives and experiences.

Fostering an Inclusive Culture

An inclusive culture is essential for creating a workplace where all employees feel valued, respected, and included. In this section, we will explore the key elements of an inclusive culture, including effective communication, unconscious bias training, and leadership support. We will also discuss the role of employee resource groups in promoting diversity and inclusion.

Addressing Issues of Discrimination and Bias

Despite efforts to create a diverse and inclusive workplace, discrimination and bias can still occur. In this section, we will provide practical strategies for addressing issues of discrimination and bias, including creating a safe reporting mechanism, conducting investigations, and implementing corrective actions. We will also discuss the importance of creating a culture of accountability to prevent discrimination and bias from occurring.

Conclusion

In conclusion, managing diversity and inclusion is essential for creating a dynamic and high-performing workplace. By understanding the importance of diversity and inclusion, creating a diverse and inclusive team, fostering an inclusive culture, and addressing issues of discrimination and bias, managers can create a workplace where all employees feel valued, respected, and included. By promoting diversity and inclusion, organizations can attract and retain top talent, increase employee engagement, and boost innovation and productivity.

Chapter 13

Strategic Planning and Execution

Strategic planning is a critical process that enables organizations to define their direction, allocate resources, and achieve their long-term objectives. As a manager's manager, it is essential to develop a comprehensive strategic plan that aligns with the organization's vision and mission. In this chapter, we will explore the four key sections of strategic planning and execution, which include developing a strategic plan, setting goals and objectives, implementing and executing the plan, and monitoring progress and making adjustments.

Developing a Strategic Plan

The first step in strategic planning is to develop a comprehensive strategic plan. This plan should include the organization's vision, mission, and values, as well as a SWOT analysis that identifies the organization's strengths, weaknesses, opportunities, and threats. The plan should also prioritize the key objectives that the organization wants to achieve.

Setting Goals and Objectives

Once the strategic plan has been developed, it is essential to set specific and measurable goals and objectives that align with the organization's vision and mission. These goals and objectives should be SMART (specific, measurable, achievable, relevant, and time-bound), and they should outline the steps that the organization needs to take to achieve its long-term objectives.

Implementing and Executing the Plan

After setting the goals and objectives, the organization needs to implement and execute the plan. This requires allocating the necessary resources, assigning responsibilities, and establishing clear communication channels to ensure that everyone is working toward the same objectives. Effective execution of the strategic plan requires collaboration, clear communication, and a willingness to adapt to changing circumstances.

Monitoring Progress and Making Adjustments

The final section of strategic planning and execution is monitoring progress and making adjustments. Regular progress monitoring ensures that the organization is making progress toward its goals and objectives. If the organization is not making sufficient progress, adjustments need to be made to the plan. This could include modifying the goals and objectives, reallocating resources, or changing the implementation strategy.

Conclusion

In conclusion, strategic planning and execution are critical components of effective management. Developing a comprehensive strategic plan, setting SMART goals and objectives, implementing and executing the plan, and monitoring progress and making adjustments are the four key sections of strategic planning and execution. By following these steps, organizations can align their resources and achieve their long-term objectives while staying competitive in the market.

Chapter 14
Managing Resources and Budgets

As a manager, it is essential to effectively manage the resources and budgets of your organization. Proper management of financial resources ensures that an organization can function efficiently and meet its goals. In this chapter, we will explore the importance of managing financial resources and provide practical strategies for creating and managing budgets, prioritizing spending, and monitoring and evaluating financial performance.

Managing Financial Resources

Managing financial resources is a critical component of effective resource management. In this section, we will discuss the importance of financial management, including the role of financial planning and forecasting. We will also explore various financial management techniques, such as financial analysis and cash flow management.

Creating and Managing Budgets

Creating and managing budgets is a crucial aspect of resource management. In this section, we will explore the steps involved in creating a budget, including identifying sources of revenue and determining expenses. We will also discuss the importance of ongoing monitoring and revision of budgets.

Prioritizing Spending

Prioritizing spending is essential to ensure that resources are used effectively and efficiently. In this section, we will discuss the importance of setting priorities when allocating resources, including how to identify critical projects and programs. We will also explore the role of performance measures in prioritizing spending decisions.

Monitoring and Evaluating Financial Performance

Monitoring and evaluating financial performance is critical to ensure that resources are being used effectively and efficiently. In this section, we will explore various methods for monitoring and evaluating financial performance, such as financial reporting, performance metrics, and benchmarking. We will also discuss the importance of ongoing evaluation and adjustment of financial management practices.

Conclusion

In conclusion, effective resource and budget management are essential for an organization's success. By managing financial resources, creating and managing budgets, prioritizing spending, and monitoring and evaluating financial performance, managers can ensure that their organizations operate efficiently and meet their goals. By promoting effective resource and budget management, organizations can maximize their resources and achieve long-term success.

Chapter 15

Conflict Resolution and Negotiation

As a manager's manager, conflict resolution and negotiation are critical skills that you need to possess. Conflicts can arise in any workplace, and how you handle them can have a significant impact on your team's productivity and overall success. In this chapter, we will explore the importance of conflict resolution and negotiation and provide practical strategies for developing conflict resolution skills, negotiating effectively to resolve conflicts, and managing union versus non-union scenarios.

Understanding Conflict and Its Impact on Teams

In this section, we will discuss the different types of conflicts that can arise in the workplace, such as interpersonal conflicts, organizational conflicts, and conflict between employees and management. We will also explore the impact of unresolved conflicts on teams, including decreased productivity, low morale, and increased turnover.

Developing Conflict Resolution Skills

In this section, we will explore practical strategies for developing conflict resolution skills, such as active listening, effective communication, and problem-solving. We will also discuss the importance of understanding cultural differences when resolving conflicts in a diverse workplace.

Negotiating Effectively to Resolve Conflicts

Negotiation is a crucial skill for managers when resolving conflicts. In this section, we will explore various negotiation techniques, including identifying common ground, using compromise and collaboration, and managing emotions during negotiations.

Mediation and Arbitration

In some cases, managers may need to involve a third party to help resolve conflicts. In this section, we will explore the concepts of mediation and arbitration, including their differences and how they can be used effectively to resolve conflicts.

Union versus Non-Union Managing

Managing conflicts in a unionized workplace can present unique challenges for managers. In this section, we will explore the differences between union and non-union environments and discuss strategies for managing conflicts in a unionized workplace.

Conclusion

In conclusion, conflict resolution and negotiation are critical skills for managers to possess. By understanding the different types of conflicts that can arise in the workplace, developing conflict resolution skills, negotiating effectively, and managing union versus non-union scenarios, managers can effectively resolve conflicts and create a positive and productive work environment. Effective conflict resolution and negotiation skills can help managers build stronger teams and achieve long-term success.

Chapter 16

Leading Innovation and Creativity

As a manager, one of your key responsibilities is to foster creativity and innovation within your team. By encouraging your team members to think outside the box, you can help your organization stay ahead of the competition and achieve long-term success. In this chapter, we will explore practical strategies for leading innovation and creativity, including encouraging creativity and innovation in the workplace, developing and implementing new ideas, managing risk and uncertainty, and celebrating and rewarding success.

Encouraging Creativity and Innovation in the Workplace

In this section, we will discuss the importance of fostering a culture of creativity and innovation within your team. We will explore practical strategies for encouraging your team members to think creatively, including brainstorming sessions, innovation workshops, and open-door policies that allow team members to share their ideas freely.

Developing and Implementing New Ideas

Once your team members have generated new ideas, it is essential to develop and implement them effectively. In this section, we will explore the process of developing new ideas, including assessing their feasibility, identifying potential challenges, and creating a plan for implementation.

Managing Risk and Uncertainty

Innovation and creativity can involve taking risks, and As a manager's manager, it is your responsibility to manage those risks effectively. In this section, we will discuss the importance of risk management in innovation and creativity, including identifying potential risks, creating contingency plans, and managing uncertainty.

Celebrating and Rewarding Success

Finally, it is crucial to celebrate and reward the successes that result from innovation and creativity. In this section, we will explore practical strategies for celebrating team successes, including public recognition, team events, and rewards programs.

Conclusion

In conclusion, leading innovation and creativity is a critical responsibility for managers. By fostering a culture of creativity and innovation, developing and implementing new ideas, managing risk and uncertainty, and celebrating and rewarding success, managers can create a positive and productive work environment that supports long-term success. Effective leadership in innovation and creativity can help managers build stronger teams and achieve their organization's goals.

Chapter 17

Ethics and Responsibility in Management

As a manager, you have a significant impact on the ethical culture of your organization. Ethical issues can arise in any workplace, and it is essential to understand how to navigate them effectively. In this chapter, we will explore practical strategies for managing ethics and responsibility in management, including understanding ethical dilemmas, developing a code of ethics and standards of conduct, making ethical decisions, and holding others accountable for ethical behavior.

Understanding Ethical Dilemmas in Management

In this section, we will explore the various ethical dilemmas that can arise in management, including conflicts of interest, confidentiality issues, and workplace harassment. We will also discuss the impact of unethical behavior on employees and the organization as a whole.

Developing a Code of Ethics and Standards of Conduct

One of the most effective ways to promote ethical behavior in the workplace is to develop a code of ethics and standards of conduct. In this section, we will discuss the key components of a code of ethics, including ethical principles, standards of conduct, and enforcement mechanisms.

Making Ethical Decisions

When faced with ethical dilemmas, managers must make difficult decisions that can have significant consequences for their organization and its stakeholders. In this section, we will explore practical strategies for making ethical decisions, including assessing the situation, considering various perspectives, and weighing the potential outcomes.

Holding Others Accountable for Ethical Behavior

Finally, it is crucial to hold others accountable for ethical behavior in the workplace. In this section, we will discuss practical strategies for promoting ethical behavior among employees, including setting expectations, training, and monitoring and enforcing ethical standards.

Conclusion

In conclusion, managing ethics and responsibility is a critical responsibility for managers. By understanding ethical dilemmas, developing a code of ethics and standards of conduct, making ethical decisions, and holding others accountable for ethical behavior, managers can create a positive and ethical work environment that supports long-term success. Effective leadership in ethics and responsibility can help managers build stronger teams and achieve their organization's goals while maintaining the highest ethical standards.

Chapter 18
Managing Virtual Teams

In recent years, managing virtual teams has become increasingly common, as many organizations shift towards remote work. While there are many benefits to managing virtual teams, such as increased flexibility and productivity, there are also unique challenges that managers must navigate. In this chapter, we will explore practical strategies for managing virtual teams, including understanding the challenges and benefits of remote work, effective communication strategies, and building trust and collaboration in virtual teams.

Challenges and Benefits of Managing Virtual Teams

In this section, we will explore the unique challenges and benefits of managing virtual teams. Some of the challenges that managers face include communication barriers, team building, and maintaining motivation and engagement. However, virtual teams can also bring many benefits, such as increased flexibility and the ability to leverage a broader talent pool.

Effective Communication Strategies for Remote Teams

Effective communication is critical to the success of virtual teams. In this section, we will explore practical strategies for communicating effectively with remote team members, including the use of video conferencing, project management tools, and email etiquette. We will also discuss the importance of establishing clear communication protocols and setting expectations for communication frequency and responsiveness.

Building Trust and Collaboration in Virtual Teams

Building trust and collaboration is essential for the success of virtual teams. In this section, we will discuss practical strategies for building trust and fostering collaboration among remote team members, including team building activities, regular check-ins, and creating opportunities for informal communication. We will also explore the role of team culture and leadership in creating a positive and productive virtual team environment.

Conclusion

In conclusion, managing virtual teams requires a unique set of skills and strategies. By understanding the challenges and benefits of remote work, communicating effectively with remote team members, and building trust and collaboration, managers can create a positive and productive virtual team environment. Effective leadership in managing virtual teams can help managers leverage the benefits of remote work while overcoming the challenges and achieving their organization's goals.

Chapter 19

Building a Strong Organizational Culture

Organizational culture plays a vital role in the success of any organization. It refers to the shared values, beliefs, behaviors, and customs that shape the way people in an organization think and act. In this chapter, we will explore practical strategies for building a strong organizational culture, including understanding the importance of culture, developing a culture that aligns with the organization's values, fostering a positive and inclusive culture, and maintaining and strengthening the culture over time.

Understanding Organizational Culture

In this section, we will explore the concept of organizational culture and its importance in shaping the behavior and attitudes of employees. We will discuss the different components of culture, including shared values, beliefs, behaviors, and customs. We will also examine the impact of culture on organizational performance, employee engagement, and retention.

Developing a Strong Culture That Aligns With the Organization's Values

In this section, we will discuss practical strategies for developing a culture that aligns with the organization's values. We will explore the role of leadership in shaping the culture and the importance of involving employees in the process. We will also discuss how to establish a set of core values that reflect the organization's mission and purpose.

Fostering a Positive and Inclusive Culture

In this section, we will discuss the importance of fostering a positive and inclusive culture. We will explore the role of diversity and inclusion in shaping the culture and the impact of a positive culture on employee engagement and retention. We will also examine practical strategies for fostering a culture of respect, trust, and collaboration.

Maintaining and Strengthening the Culture Over Time

In this section, we will discuss practical strategies for maintaining and strengthening the culture over time. We will examine the role of communication in reinforcing the culture and the importance of measuring and monitoring the culture regularly. We will also discuss the impact of leadership changes, mergers, and acquisitions on the culture and how to manage these changes effectively.

Conclusion

In conclusion, building a strong organizational culture is a crucial factor in achieving organizational success. By understanding the importance of culture, developing a culture that aligns with the organization's values, fostering a positive and inclusive culture, and maintaining and strengthening the culture over time, organizations can create a culture that attracts and retains top talent, drives performance, and achieves its strategic goals.

Chapter 20

Managing Time and Priorities

Time is a finite resource, and effective time management is critical for achieving success in any organization. In this chapter, we will explore practical strategies for managing time and priorities, including managing time effectively, setting priorities and goals, delegating tasks and responsibilities, and eliminating time-wasting activities.

Managing Time Effectively

In this section, we will discuss practical strategies for managing time effectively. We will explore the importance of creating a daily schedule, setting realistic deadlines, and avoiding procrastination. We will also examine the impact of interruptions and distractions on productivity and discuss practical strategies for minimizing their impact.

Setting Priorities and Goals

In this section, we will discuss practical strategies for setting priorities and goals. We will explore the importance of aligning goals with the organization's mission and vision, prioritizing tasks based on their importance and urgency, and breaking down long-term goals into smaller, achievable tasks. We will also examine the role of goal-setting in increasing motivation and productivity.

Delegating Tasks and Responsibilities

In this section, we will discuss practical strategies for delegating tasks and responsibilities. We will explore the importance of delegating tasks based on the skills and expertise of team members, providing clear instructions and expectations, and establishing accountability. We will also examine the impact of effective delegation on productivity, employee development, and team collaboration.

Eliminating Time-Wasting Activities

In this section, we will discuss practical strategies for eliminating time-wasting activities. We will explore the impact of unproductive activities such as excessive meetings, email overload, and multitasking on productivity and discuss practical strategies for minimizing their impact. We will also examine the importance of taking breaks and prioritizing self-care to improve productivity and reduce burnout.

Conclusion

In conclusion, effective time management and prioritization are essential for achieving success in any organization. By managing time effectively, setting priorities and goals, delegating tasks and responsibilities, and eliminating time-wasting activities, organizations can improve productivity, reduce stress, and achieve their strategic goals.

Chapter 21

Leading and Managing Projects

Managing projects is a critical skill for any manager, as projects are often the vehicle through which an organization achieves its strategic goals. In this chapter, we will explore practical strategies for leading and managing projects, including understanding the project management process, defining project scope, objectives, and timelines, developing a project plan and budget, and managing project risks and issues.

Understanding the Project Management Process

In this section, we will discuss the project management process and its key stages. We will explore the importance of initiating, planning, executing, monitoring and controlling, and closing a project, and discuss the key activities and deliverables associated with each stage. We will also examine the role of project management methodologies such as Agile and Waterfall in managing projects.

Defining Project Scope, Objectives, and Timelines

In this section, we will discuss practical strategies for defining project scope, objectives, and timelines. We will explore the importance of aligning project objectives with the organization's strategic goals, defining the scope of work and deliverables, and setting realistic timelines. We will also examine the impact of poor project scoping on project outcomes and discuss practical strategies for avoiding scope creep.

Developing a Project Plan and Budget

In this section, we will discuss practical strategies for developing a project plan and budget. We will explore the importance of developing a detailed project plan that outlines the tasks, milestones, and deliverables, as well as identifying the resources and budget required to complete the project. We will also examine the role of project management software in planning and tracking project progress.

Managing Project Risks and Issues

In this section, we will discuss practical strategies for managing project risks and issues. We will explore the importance of identifying and assessing project risks, developing contingency plans, and communicating risks and issues to stakeholders. We will also examine the impact of poor risk management on project outcomes and discuss practical strategies for mitigating risks and resolving issues.

Conclusion

In conclusion, leading and managing projects requires a combination of technical skills, project management methodologies, and effective communication and leadership skills. By understanding the project management process, defining project scope, objectives, and timelines, developing a project plan and budget, and managing project risks and issues, organizations can successfully deliver projects that achieve their strategic goals.

Chapter 22

Emotional Intelligence for Managers

Effective management requires not only technical and operational skills, but also emotional intelligence. Emotional intelligence is the ability to understand and manage one's own emotions, as well as to perceive and influence the emotions of others. In this chapter, we will explore the importance of emotional intelligence for managers and provide practical strategies for developing emotional intelligence skills.

Understanding Emotional Intelligence

Emotional intelligence is a set of competencies that enable individuals to recognize and understand their own emotions, as well as the emotions of others. This includes the ability to manage emotions effectively and to use emotions to guide thinking and behavior. Emotional intelligence can be broken down into five key components:

Self-awareness: the ability to recognize and understand one's own emotions, strengths, and weaknesses.

Self-regulation: the ability to manage and control one's own emotions, impulses, and behaviors.

Motivation: the ability to use emotions to drive and sustain motivation and to pursue goals with energy and persistence.

Empathy: the ability to recognize and understand the emotions of others and to respond appropriately.

Social skills: the ability to build and maintain positive relationships with others and to communicate effectively.

Developing Self-Awareness and Self-Regulation

Self-awareness and self-regulation are critical components of emotional intelligence. Developing self-awareness involves recognizing and understanding one's own emotions, thoughts, and behaviors. This can be accomplished through activities such as mindfulness, journaling, and seeking feedback from others. Self-regulation involves managing one's own emotions, impulses, and behaviors in order to achieve desired outcomes. Strategies for improving self-regulation skills include practicing mindfulness, developing a plan for managing emotions, and seeking support from colleagues or mentors.

Building Empathy and Social Skills

Empathy and social skills are also important components of emotional intelligence. Empathy involves understanding the emotions and perspectives of others, and responding appropriately. Strategies for developing empathy include active listening, perspective-taking, and seeking feedback from others. Social skills involve building and maintaining positive relationships with others, communicating effectively, and working collaboratively. Strategies for developing social skills include building a strong network, practicing effective communication, and seeking opportunities for collaboration.

Managing Emotions in the Workplace

Managing emotions effectively in the workplace is critical for success As a manager's manager. This includes being able to handle stress and pressure, manage conflicts and difficult situations, and build a positive and productive work environment. Strategies for managing emotions in the workplace include practicing self-care, setting boundaries, seeking support from colleagues, and using emotions to build positive relationships.

In conclusion, emotional intelligence is an essential skill set for effective management. By developing self-awareness, self-regulation, empathy, and social skills, managers can build positive relationships with colleagues and stakeholders, motivate and engage their teams, and create a productive and positive work environment.

Chapter 23
Leading and Managing in Crisis

Introduction: Crises can strike any organization at any time, from natural disasters and accidents to financial crises and cyber-attacks. Effective leadership and management are critical in times of crisis to minimize damage, ensure business continuity, and protect the organization's reputation. This chapter will discuss the key strategies and best practices for leading and managing in a crisis situation.

Section 1: Preparing for and Managing Crises

- Understanding different types of crises and their potential impact on the organization
- Developing a crisis management plan and identifying key crisis management team members
- Conducting regular risk assessments and updating the crisis management plan accordingly
- Establishing communication protocols for crisis situations, including emergency notifications and escalation procedures

Section 2: Developing Crisis Communication Plans

- The importance of effective communication during a crisis

- Identifying key stakeholders and their information needs
- Developing messaging and communication channels for different audiences
- Preparing for media inquiries and developing key messages
- Conducting crisis communication drills and exercises to test the plan

Section 3: Leading and Managing Teams in Times of Crisis

- The role of leaders and managers in a crisis situation
- Providing clear direction and guidance to team members
- Communicating with empathy and transparency to address concerns and manage expectations
- Ensuring team members have the necessary resources and support to perform their roles
- Monitoring team performance and providing feedback and recognition as needed

Section 4: Learning from Past Crises to Improve Future Responses

- Conducting post-crisis reviews and debriefs to identify areas for improvement
- Updating the crisis management plan based on lessons learned
- Incorporating feedback from team members and stakeholders into the crisis management plan
- Providing training and resources to help team members prepare for future crises

Conclusion:

Leading and managing in a crisis situation can be challenging, but by preparing ahead of time, developing effective communication plans, and providing strong leadership and support to team members, organizations can minimize the impact of crises and emerge stronger and more resilient. It is important to continuously learn from past experiences and update crisis management plans accordingly to be better prepared for future crises.

Chapter 24

Managing and Leveraging Technology

Technology has become an integral part of modern business, with almost every aspect of a company's operations relying on technology in some form. As a manager, it is essential to understand the impact of technology on business and how to manage and leverage it effectively.

Understanding the impact of technology on business

- The role of technology in modern business
- How technology has changed the way we work
- The benefits and drawbacks of technology in the workplace
- Managing technology resources and infrastructure

Developing and maintaining a technology strategy

- Ensuring adequate resources are allocated to technology
- Managing and securing company data and information
- Overseeing the implementation and maintenance of hardware and software
- Leveraging technology to improve efficiency and productivity

Identifying areas where technology can improve operations

- Implementing technology solutions to streamline processes
- Automating repetitive tasks to increase efficiency
- Using technology to better analyze and interpret data
- Staying current with technological advances

Keeping up-to-date with new technologies and trends

Encouraging employees to stay informed about technological advances

Evaluating and adopting new technologies when appropriate

Balancing the benefits of new technology with the cost and potential risks

In conclusion, managing and leveraging technology is a critical part of modern business management. By understanding the impact of technology on business, managing technology resources and infrastructure, leveraging technology to improve efficiency and productivity, and staying current with technological advances, managers can ensure their organization stays competitive and efficient in the ever-evolving technological landscape.

Chapter 25

Global Leadership and Management

In today's globalized world, leaders and managers must have the skills and knowledge to manage and lead teams from diverse cultural backgrounds. The following sections provide insights into understanding cultural differences and their impact on management, developing a global mindset, managing and leading teams in different cultures, and communicating effectively across cultural boundaries.

1. Understanding Cultural Differences and Their Impact on Management

   Culture plays a significant role in shaping attitudes, behaviors, and values. Understanding the cultural differences of employees, clients, and partners is essential for effective leadership and management. In this section, we will explore the impact of cultural differences on management styles, decision-making, communication, and conflict resolution.

2. Developing a Global Mindset

   A global mindset is a crucial attribute for leaders and managers who work in international settings. Developing a global mindset involves being aware of cultural differences, being open-minded, and demonstrating flexibility. This section will provide insights into the essential skills and competencies required to develop a global mindset.

3. Managing and Leading Teams in Different Cultures

   Managing and leading teams from different cultures require a specific set of skills and competencies. This section will provide guidance on how to manage and lead teams effectively in different cultures, including developing a communication strategy, setting expectations, building trust, and managing conflicts.

4. Communicating Effectively Across Cultural Boundaries

   Communication is a vital skill for effective leadership and management. However, communicating across cultural boundaries can be challenging. This section will provide insights into the different communication styles and cultural norms that may impact communication. It will also provide practical tips on how to communicate effectively across cultural boundaries.

   In conclusion, global leadership and management require a unique set of skills and competencies. Leaders and managers who understand the impact of cultural differences on management, develop a global mindset, manage and lead teams effectively in different cultures, and communicate effectively across cultural boundaries will be better equipped to succeed in today's globalized world.

Chapter 26

Leading and Managing Change in a Digital Age

As businesses increasingly rely on technology and digital solutions, it becomes essential for leaders and managers to understand the impact of digital transformation on businesses. This chapter will explore the various aspects of leading and managing change in a digital age, including developing strategies for digital change, leading and managing change in a digital environment, and preparing employees for digital change.

Understanding the Impact of Digital Transformation on Businesses

Digital transformation refers to the integration of digital technologies into all aspects of a business, fundamentally changing how it operates and delivers value to customers. The impact of digital transformation on businesses can be significant, affecting everything from business models and customer engagement to internal operations and employee skill sets.

One of the primary benefits of digital transformation is the ability to improve customer experiences by providing personalized and convenient services. For example, the rise of mobile devices has enabled businesses to connect with customers anytime and anywhere, while digital platforms allow for real-time interactions and transactions. In addition, digital technologies can streamline internal processes, making operations more efficient and reducing costs.

However, the rapid pace of digital change can also present challenges for businesses, especially those that are slow to adopt new technologies. Failure to keep up with digital transformation can result in lost opportunities and decreased competitiveness.

Developing Strategies for Digital Change

To successfully navigate digital transformation, businesses must develop strategies that are tailored to their specific needs and goals. This involves assessing the current state of the organization, identifying areas where digital technologies can be implemented, and setting achievable objectives.

One key strategy for digital change is to prioritize investments in areas that will have the most significant impact on business performance. This may involve focusing on areas such as customer engagement, data analytics, or automation, depending on the business's specific needs.

Another important strategy is to build a culture of innovation that encourages experimentation and risk-taking. This involves creating an environment where employees are empowered to propose and test new ideas, with a focus on learning from failures and using feedback to improve.

Leading and Managing Change in a Digital Environment

Leading and managing change in a digital environment requires a different approach than traditional change management. In addition to the usual challenges of managing change, such as resistance to change and uncertainty, digital transformation requires leaders to navigate the complexities of new technologies and the potential impact on existing business models.

One key aspect of leading digital change is to create a sense of urgency and a shared vision for the future of the organization. This involves communicating the need for change, the benefits of digital transformation, and the specific goals and objectives of the change initiative.

Another important aspect is to involve employees and stakeholders in the change process. This includes providing training and support for new technologies, as well as creating opportunities for feedback and collaboration. In addition, leaders must be prepared to address resistance to change and potential disruptions to existing processes.

Preparing Employees for Digital Change

As digital transformation continues to impact businesses, it is essential to prepare employees for the changes ahead. This involves not only providing training and support for new technologies but also developing the necessary skills and mindsets to thrive in a digital environment.

One key area of focus is developing digital literacy, or the ability to use digital technologies effectively. This may involve providing training on specific tools and platforms, as well as encouraging employees to explore new technologies on their own.

In addition, employees must develop critical thinking skills and adaptability to navigate the complex and rapidly changing digital landscape. This includes the ability to analyze data, collaborate with others, and learn new skills quickly.

Conclusion

Digital transformation is reshaping businesses across industries, presenting both opportunities and challenges for leaders and managers. To successfully navigate this change, businesses must develop strategies that are tailored to their specific needs and goals, prioritize investments in areas that will have the most significant impact on business performance, and build a culture of innovation. Leaders must create a sense of urgency and a shared vision for digital change, involve employees and stakeholders in the change process, and prepare employees for the skills and mindset needed to thrive in a digital environment. By doing so, businesses can successfully lead and manage change in a digital age, creating a competitive advantage and driving growth and innovation.

Chapter 27

Ethics and Social Responsibility in a Global Context

As businesses operate in an increasingly globalized and interconnected world, it becomes essential for leaders and managers to understand the impact of their actions on society and the environment. This chapter will explore the various aspects of ethics and social responsibility in a global context, including understanding the impact of business on society and the environment, developing sustainable and socially responsible practices, making ethical decisions in a global context, and balancing profits and social responsibility.

Understanding the Impact of Business on Society and the Environment

Businesses have a significant impact on society and the environment, from the products and services they offer to the way they operate and interact with stakeholders. Some of the negative impacts of business on society and the environment include pollution, exploitation of workers, and disregard for human rights.

On the other hand, businesses can also have a positive impact on society and the environment by creating jobs, investing in communities, and promoting sustainable practices. To maximize positive impact and minimize negative impact, it is essential for businesses to understand their role in society and the environment and to adopt practices that align with their values and goals.

Developing Sustainable and Socially Responsible Practices

To operate in a socially responsible and sustainable way, businesses must adopt practices that consider the impact of their actions on the environment, society, and stakeholders. This involves developing policies and procedures that promote sustainable practices, including reducing waste and emissions, conserving resources, and promoting social justice.

In addition, businesses must consider the impact of their supply chain on the environment and society, including the conditions of workers and the sourcing of raw materials. This requires engaging with suppliers and partners to ensure they meet the same standards and values as the business.

Making Ethical Decisions in a Global Context

As businesses operate in a global context, they must navigate different cultural, legal, and ethical frameworks. This can present challenges in making ethical decisions that align with the business's values and goals.

To make ethical decisions in a global context, businesses must consider the cultural and social norms of the countries in which they operate, as well as the laws and regulations that govern their actions. In addition, businesses must consider the impact of their decisions on stakeholders, including customers, employees, and the broader community.

Balancing Profits and Social Responsibility

One of the challenges of social responsibility is balancing the interests of stakeholders with the need to generate profits. While businesses have a responsibility to act in a socially responsible way, they must also remain profitable to sustain operations and provide value to shareholders.

To balance profits and social responsibility, businesses must adopt a long-term perspective that considers the impact of their actions on stakeholders over time. This may involve investing in sustainable practices that may not yield immediate financial benefits but contribute to long-term profitability.

Conclusion

As businesses operate in an increasingly interconnected and complex world, it becomes essential for leaders and managers to understand the impact of their actions on society and the environment. By developing sustainable and socially responsible practices, making ethical decisions in a global context, and balancing profits and social responsibility, businesses can contribute to a more just and sustainable future while also creating value for stakeholders.

Chapter 28

Building and Maintaining a Personal Brand

As a manager's manager, it is essential to establish a personal brand that communicates your values, goals, and expertise. A strong personal brand can help you stand out in a competitive job market, build trust with colleagues and stakeholders, and establish yourself as a thought leader in your field. This chapter will explore the importance of personal branding in management, developing a personal brand that aligns with your values and goals, building and maintaining an online presence, and networking to support your personal brand.

Understanding the Importance of Personal Branding in Management

Personal branding is the process of defining and communicating your unique value proposition as a professional. In management, a personal brand can help you establish credibility and influence, build relationships with stakeholders, and differentiate yourself from competitors.

A strong personal brand can also help you build a reputation for excellence, increase your visibility and opportunities for advancement, and attract new clients and business opportunities.

Developing a Personal Brand that Aligns with Your Values and Goals

To develop a personal brand that resonates with your audience and aligns with your values and goals, it is essential to understand your strengths, expertise, and unique value proposition. This involves conducting a self-assessment of your skills and experience, identifying your core values and passions, and defining your target audience.

Once you have defined your personal brand, it is important to communicate it effectively through your messaging, marketing materials, and personal interactions.

Building and Maintaining an Online Presence

In today's digital age, building and maintaining an online presence is essential to establishing a strong personal brand. This includes creating a professional website, maintaining active social media profiles, and participating in online communities and forums relevant to your field.

To build and maintain an effective online presence, it is important to create high-quality content that reflects your expertise and adds value to your audience. This can include blog posts, videos, podcasts, and other forms of content that showcase your unique insights and perspectives.

Networking and Building Relationships to Support Your Personal Brand

Finally, networking and building relationships is essential to building and maintaining a strong personal brand. This involves connecting with colleagues, mentors, and industry leaders to learn from their experiences, build trust, and expand your professional network.

To build effective relationships, it is important to be proactive, genuine, and generous with your time and expertise. This can involve attending industry events and conferences, joining professional organizations, and participating in networking groups and mentorship programs.

Conclusion

In today's competitive business environment, building and maintaining a strong personal brand is essential to establishing credibility, building relationships, and achieving professional success. By understanding the importance of personal branding, developing a personal brand that aligns with your values and goals, building and maintaining an online presence, and networking to support your personal brand, you can establish yourself as a thought leader and achieve your professional goals.

Chapter 29

Leading and Managing Diversity and Inclusion

As workplaces become increasingly diverse, it is essential for managers to understand the importance of diversity and inclusion in creating a thriving, productive environment. This chapter will explore the importance of diversity and inclusion in the workplace, creating an inclusive workplace culture, managing diverse teams effectively, addressing bias and discrimination in the workplace, and dealing with nepotism in the workplace.

Understanding the Importance of Diversity and Inclusion in the Workplace

Diversity and inclusion are essential to creating a workplace culture that supports innovation, creativity, and collaboration. By embracing diversity in all its forms, including gender, race, ethnicity, age, sexual orientation, and abilities, organizations can leverage the unique perspectives and experiences of their employees to drive innovation and create value.

Creating an Inclusive Workplace Culture

To create an inclusive workplace culture, it is essential for managers to embrace diversity in all its forms, promote open communication and collaboration, and actively seek out and address bias and discrimination. This can involve providing diversity training for employees, creating policies that support diversity and inclusion, and promoting a culture of respect and inclusion.

Managing Diverse Teams Effectively

Managing diverse teams requires a nuanced approach that recognizes the unique perspectives and experiences of each team member. This can involve creating a culture of trust and transparency, promoting open communication and collaboration, and providing opportunities for team members to share their perspectives and experiences.

To manage diverse teams effectively, it is also important to provide training and support for managers and team members, promote inclusivity and respect, and address conflicts and challenges in a timely and constructive manner.

Addressing Bias and Discrimination in the Workplace

Bias and discrimination can have a significant impact on workplace culture and productivity, and it is essential for managers to proactively address these issues. This can involve creating policies and procedures that support diversity and inclusion, providing training and education for employees, and promoting a culture of respect and inclusivity.

Managers should also be aware of their own biases and work to address them, promote open communication and feedback, and take swift action to address instances of bias and discrimination in the workplace.

Nepotism in the Workplace

Nepotism, or the practice of favoring relatives or friends in the workplace, can create a toxic culture of favoritism and undermine productivity and morale. To address nepotism in the workplace, managers should create policies and procedures that promote fairness and transparency, ensure that hiring and promotion decisions are based on merit and qualifications rather than personal connections, and provide training and education for employees on the impact of nepotism on workplace culture.

Conclusion

In today's diverse workplace, creating a culture of inclusion and respect is essential to driving innovation, productivity, and success. By understanding the importance of diversity and inclusion, creating an inclusive workplace culture, managing diverse teams effectively, addressing bias and discrimination, and addressing nepotism in the workplace, managers can create a culture of inclusivity and respect that supports employee engagement and drives business success.

Chapter 30

Building and Managing Strategic Partnerships

Strategic partnerships can be a powerful tool for organizations looking to achieve their business objectives and create value for their stakeholders. This chapter will explore the benefits of strategic partnerships, identifying and selecting strategic partners, negotiating and managing partnerships effectively, and evaluating the success of strategic partnerships.

Understanding the Benefits of Strategic Partnerships

Strategic partnerships offer a range of benefits for organizations, including access to new markets, customers, and technologies, increased operational efficiencies, and reduced costs. By partnering with other organizations, companies can leverage their strengths and capabilities to create new opportunities and generate value for their stakeholders.

Identifying and Selecting Strategic Partners

To identify and select strategic partners, companies should consider their business objectives, target markets, and strategic priorities. This may involve conducting market research, identifying potential partners through networking and industry events, and evaluating potential partners based on their capabilities, track record, and alignment with the company's values and goals.

Negotiating and Managing Partnerships Effectively

To negotiate and manage partnerships effectively, companies should establish clear goals and expectations, define the scope and duration of the partnership, and develop a governance structure and communication plan. This may involve developing a partnership agreement that outlines the responsibilities and expectations of each partner, establishing a project management team to oversee the partnership, and providing ongoing support and resources to ensure the success of the partnership.

Evaluating the Success of Strategic Partnerships

To evaluate the success of strategic partnerships, companies should establish clear performance metrics and regularly track and evaluate the partnership's progress. This may involve conducting regular performance reviews, soliciting feedback from stakeholders, and conducting periodic assessments of the partnership's impact on the company's business objectives.

Conclusion

Building and managing strategic partnerships can be a powerful tool for organizations looking to achieve their business objectives and create value for their stakeholders. By understanding the benefits of strategic partnerships, identifying and selecting strategic partners, negotiating and managing partnerships effectively, and evaluating the success of strategic partnerships, companies can create successful partnerships that drive growth and innovation.

Chapter 31

Leading and Managing Innovation

Innovation is critical for businesses to stay competitive and meet the ever-changing needs of customers. This chapter will explore the importance of innovation in businesses, developing a culture of innovation, generating and implementing new ideas, and managing risks and challenges associated with innovation.

Understanding the Importance of Innovation in Businesses

Innovation is the key to staying ahead of the competition and driving growth in today's fast-paced business environment. Businesses that fail to innovate risk becoming irrelevant and losing market share. Therefore, innovation must be a core component of every organization's strategy.

Developing a Culture of Innovation

Creating a culture of innovation requires leadership support and a commitment to risk-taking and experimentation. Leaders must encourage employees to generate and share new ideas, provide resources and support for innovation initiatives, and reward innovative thinking and behaviors. It is also important to foster a culture of collaboration and openness, where employees are encouraged to share ideas and work together to solve problems.

Generating and Implementing New Ideas

Generating new ideas can come from a variety of sources, such as employees, customers, and partnerships with other organizations. Companies can also create innovation labs or incubators to foster creativity and experimentation. Once ideas are generated, it is important to evaluate and prioritize them based on their potential impact and feasibility. Ideas can then be implemented using agile project management methodologies and continuous improvement processes.

Managing Risks and Challenges Associated with Innovation

Innovation comes with risks and challenges, such as uncertainty, failure, and resistance to change. Companies can mitigate these risks by establishing a structured process for innovation, setting clear goals and performance metrics, and building a culture that encourages experimentation and learning from failure. It is also important to communicate the benefits of innovation to stakeholders and address any concerns or resistance to change.

Conclusion

Innovation is critical for businesses to stay ahead of the competition and meet the evolving needs of customers. By developing a culture of innovation, generating and implementing new ideas, and managing risks and challenges associated with innovation, companies can drive growth and remain relevant in today's rapidly changing business environment.

Chapter 32
Managing Remote Teams

The COVID-19 pandemic has accelerated the trend towards remote work, making it more important than ever for managers to effectively manage remote teams. This chapter will explore the challenges and benefits of remote work, managing remote teams effectively, building trust and communication in a remote environment, and developing policies and practices to support remote work.

Understanding the Challenges and Benefits of Remote Work

Remote work presents both challenges and benefits for businesses. While it provides employees with more flexibility and reduces costs associated with office space and commuting, it also poses challenges related to communication, collaboration, and managing performance. It is important for managers to understand both the benefits and challenges of remote work to effectively manage remote teams.

Managing Remote Teams Effectively

To manage remote teams effectively, managers must establish clear expectations and communication channels, ensure that employees have the necessary tools and resources to work remotely, and provide regular feedback and recognition. It is also important to set goals and monitor performance, provide opportunities for professional development and career growth, and foster a culture of trust and collaboration.

Building Trust and Communication in a Remote Environment

Building trust and communication in a remote environment is critical for the success of remote teams. Managers must establish regular communication channels, encourage open and honest communication, and use video conferencing and other technologies to maintain regular face-to-face interactions. It is also important to establish clear guidelines and expectations for communication and provide training and support to employees on how to effectively communicate in a remote environment.

Developing Policies and Practices to Support Remote Work

To support remote work, companies must develop policies and practices that address issues related to cybersecurity, data privacy, and employee well-being. This includes establishing clear guidelines for data access and protection, providing employees with ergonomic workspaces, and promoting work-life balance. It is also important to provide training and support to employees on how to effectively work remotely and ensure that policies and practices are regularly reviewed and updated.

Conclusion

Managing remote teams requires a different approach than managing traditional office-based teams. By understanding the challenges and benefits of remote work, managing remote teams effectively, building trust and communication in a remote environment, and developing policies and practices to support remote work, managers can successfully lead remote teams and drive business results.

Chapter 33

Crisis Management and Business Continuity

Crisis situations can arise unexpectedly in any business, making it crucial for managers to develop a crisis management plan and ensure business continuity. This chapter will explore the importance of crisis management and business continuity, developing a crisis management plan, managing crises effectively, and maintaining business continuity during crises.

Understanding Crisis Management and Business Continuity

Crisis management involves identifying potential risks and developing strategies to mitigate them. Business continuity refers to the ability of a business to continue its operations during and after a crisis. Both crisis management and business continuity are essential for minimizing the impact of a crisis on a business and ensuring its long-term sustainability.

Developing a Crisis Management Plan

To effectively manage a crisis, businesses must develop a crisis management plan that outlines key roles and responsibilities, communication protocols, and contingency plans. The plan should also address potential risks and provide guidance on how to respond to different types of crises. It is important to regularly review and update the plan to ensure it remains relevant and effective.

Managing Crises Effectively

During a crisis, effective management is critical to minimize its impact on the business. This involves activating the crisis management plan, communicating regularly with stakeholders, prioritizing the safety and well-being of employees and customers, and making swift and decisive decisions. It is also important to maintain transparency and provide timely updates to stakeholders.

Maintaining Business Continuity During Crises

Maintaining business continuity during a crisis requires a combination of planning and agility. This includes establishing remote work policies and procedures, implementing backup systems and data recovery plans, and developing contingency plans for supply chain disruptions. It is important to regularly test these plans and adjust them as necessary.

Conclusion

Crisis management and business continuity are essential for any business to weather unexpected disruptions. By understanding the importance of crisis management and business continuity, developing a crisis management plan, managing crises effectively, and maintaining business continuity during crises, managers can ensure the long-term sustainability of their business.

Chapter 34

Leading and Managing in a VUCA World

The world we live in today is increasingly volatile, uncertain, complex, and ambiguous (VUCA). This chapter will explore the meaning of VUCA, developing strategies to manage VUCA challenges, leading and managing teams effectively in a VUCA world, and anticipating and adapting to change.

The Meaning of VUCA

The term VUCA was originally coined by the US military to describe the challenges faced by soldiers in a post-Cold War world. Today, it has become a widely used term in business to describe the unpredictable and rapidly changing environment that businesses operate in. Volatility refers to the speed and magnitude of changes, uncertainty relates to the lack of predictability and understanding of events, complexity refers to the interconnectedness and multitude of factors, and ambiguity refers to the lack of clarity and multiple interpretations.

Developing Strategies to Manage VUCA Challenges

To manage VUCA challenges, businesses need to develop strategies that are agile and flexible. This includes developing scenario planning techniques to prepare for a range of possible outcomes, building adaptive and resilient systems and processes, and focusing on innovation and experimentation to remain competitive. It is also essential to develop a culture of continuous learning and development to enable teams to respond effectively to new challenges.

Leading and Managing Teams Effectively in a VUCA World

To lead and manage teams effectively in a VUCA world, leaders need to adopt an agile and flexible approach. This includes fostering a culture of open communication and collaboration, empowering employees to make decisions and take ownership of their work, and encouraging experimentation and risk-taking. Leaders should also prioritize developing their emotional intelligence and adaptability skills to be able to navigate complex and uncertain situations.

Anticipating and Adapting to Change

In a VUCA world, change is constant, and businesses must anticipate and adapt to it to remain competitive. This includes developing foresight and scanning techniques to identify emerging trends and potential disruptions, building a culture of innovation and experimentation to test new ideas, and developing an agile and flexible approach to responding to change. Businesses must also prioritize employee development and training to ensure they have the skills and knowledge to adapt to new challenges.

Conclusion

Leading and managing in a VUCA world requires businesses to adopt an agile and flexible approach to managing challenges and adapting to change. By understanding the meaning of VUCA, developing strategies to manage VUCA challenges, leading and managing teams effectively, and anticipating and adapting to change, businesses can navigate the unpredictable and rapidly changing environment and remain competitive in the long term.

Chapter 35

Managing and Mitigating Risk

Businesses face a variety of risks that can impact their operations, financial performance, and reputation. This chapter will explore the different types of business risks, developing a risk management plan, identifying and assessing risks, and implementing risk mitigation strategies.

Understanding the Types of Business Risks

Business risks can be classified into several categories, including strategic risks, financial risks, operational risks, compliance risks, and reputational risks. Strategic risks refer to risks related to changes in the business environment and the ability to adapt to those changes. Financial risks include risks related to financial performance, such as fluctuations in exchange rates or interest rates. Operational risks refer to risks related to day-to-day business operations, such as supply chain disruptions or equipment failure. Compliance risks refer to risks related to complying with laws and regulations, and reputational risks refer to risks related to the company's image and reputation.

Developing a Risk Management Plan

A risk management plan outlines the process for identifying, assessing, and managing risks. It should include a risk management framework that outlines the roles and responsibilities of team members, the risk assessment process, risk mitigation strategies, and a risk management reporting system. The plan should be regularly reviewed and updated to ensure it remains effective and relevant.

Identifying and Assessing Risks

Identifying and assessing risks is a critical step in risk management. It involves identifying potential risks, analyzing the likelihood and impact of each risk, and prioritizing risks based on their level of importance. The risk assessment process should involve input from all relevant stakeholders, including employees, customers, suppliers, and regulators.

Implementing Risk Mitigation Strategies

Once risks have been identified and assessed, it is important to implement risk mitigation strategies to minimize the impact of potential risks. Risk mitigation strategies can include developing contingency plans, diversifying supply chains, implementing security measures, and purchasing insurance. It is also important to regularly monitor and evaluate the effectiveness of risk mitigation strategies to ensure they remain relevant and effective.

Conclusion

Managing and mitigating business risks is essential for ensuring the long-term success and sustainability of a business. By understanding the types of business risks, developing a risk management plan, identifying and assessing risks, and implementing risk mitigation strategies, businesses can effectively manage potential risks and minimize their impact. Regularly reviewing and updating the risk management plan is crucial to ensure it remains relevant and effective in an ever-changing business environment.

Chapter 36
Managing and Resolving Conflict

Conflict is an inevitable part of any workplace, and it can have a negative impact on productivity, morale, and overall workplace culture. This chapter will explore the causes and types of conflict in the workplace, developing conflict resolution strategies, managing and resolving conflict effectively, and preventing and minimizing conflict in the workplace.

Understanding the Causes and Types of Conflict in the Workplace

Conflict in the workplace can arise from a variety of sources, including differences in personalities, values, opinions, and goals. Common types of conflict in the workplace include interpersonal conflict, role conflict, resource conflict, and task conflict. Interpersonal conflict arises from differences in personalities or communication styles, while role conflict arises from conflicting expectations between individuals or departments. Resource conflict arises from competition for limited resources, and task conflict arises from differences in how to approach a particular task or project.

Developing Conflict Resolution Strategies

Developing effective conflict resolution strategies involves understanding the causes and types of conflict, developing communication and negotiation skills, and promoting a culture of respect and open communication. Conflict resolution strategies can include mediation, arbitration, negotiation, and collaboration. It is important to approach conflict resolution with a positive attitude, active listening skills, and an open mind.

Managing and Resolving Conflict Effectively

Managing and resolving conflict effectively involves recognizing the signs of conflict early on, addressing the issue in a timely and respectful manner, and working collaboratively to find a solution that satisfies all parties involved. Effective conflict resolution requires clear communication, active listening, and a willingness to compromise.

Preventing and Minimizing Conflict in the Workplace

Preventing and minimizing conflict in the workplace involves creating a culture of open communication, promoting respect and understanding among team members, and establishing clear expectations and guidelines for behavior. Effective conflict prevention strategies include providing training and development opportunities, encouraging teamwork and collaboration, and fostering a positive workplace culture.

Conclusion

Conflict in the workplace is inevitable, but it can be managed and resolved effectively with the right strategies and mindset. By understanding the causes and types of conflict, developing conflict resolution strategies, managing and resolving conflict effectively, and preventing and minimizing conflict in the workplace, businesses can create a positive and productive workplace culture. It is important to approach conflict resolution with a positive attitude, active listening skills, and a willingness to compromise. Creating a culture of open communication, promoting respect and understanding among team members, and establishing clear expectations and guidelines for behavior can also help prevent and minimize conflict in the workplace.

Chapter 37

Understanding Management Across Cultures: A Global Perspective

Introduction: Culture and Management Style

Culture shapes the way people perceive and behave in the world, including how they approach management and leadership. As global business continues to grow, it is essential to understand and appreciate the diversity of management styles across cultures. This chapter will explore different management styles and their cultural influences.

Western Management Styles: Individualism and Egalitarianism

Western management styles tend to emphasize individualism and egalitarianism. In these cultures, managers are expected to be open and communicative with employees, and decision-making processes are often democratic. Performance is measured by individual achievement and merit, and employees are encouraged to take initiative and responsibility.

Eastern Management Styles: Hierarchy and Collectivism

In contrast, Eastern management styles tend to be more hierarchical and collectivistic. These cultures value respect for authority, and managers are often expected to be authoritarian and paternalistic. Decision-making processes tend to be centralized, and consensus is often sought through informal networks. Performance is often measured in terms of group achievement and loyalty to the organization.

Middle Eastern Management Styles: Religion and Tribalism

In Middle Eastern cultures, religion and tribalism often influence management styles. Managers may be expected to act as paternalistic leaders who provide guidance and protection for their employees. Decision-making processes tend to be centralized, and hierarchy is often based on age and experience. Personal relationships and trust are essential in these cultures, and negotiations may take longer as trust is built.

South Asia Management Styles: Bangladesh, Bhutan, India, Maldives, Nepal, Pakistan, Sri Lanka, and Afghanistan

South Asia is a culturally diverse region with distinct management styles that reflect the region's unique history, religion, and social structures. In this section, we will explore the management styles of Bangladesh, Bhutan, India, Maldives, Nepal, Pakistan, Sri Lanka, and Afghanistan.

In Bangladesh, management is typically hierarchical, with a clear chain of command and emphasis on authority and respect for elders. There is also a strong focus on building personal relationships and maintaining harmony in the workplace.

Bhutanese management style is heavily influenced by the country's Buddhist values, which emphasize compassion, harmony, and balance. There is a strong emphasis on teamwork, and decision-making is often based on consensus.

Indian management style varies depending on the region and industry, but generally, there is a strong emphasis on hierarchy and respect for authority. There is also a focus on building personal relationships and trust, and decision-making often involves consultation with superiors.

Maldivian management style is influenced by the country's Islamic values, which emphasize respect for authority and hierarchy. Decision-making is often centralized, with top-level managers making key decisions.

In Nepal, management is hierarchical, with a clear chain of command and emphasis on authority and respect for elders. There is also a strong emphasis on building personal relationships and maintaining harmony in the workplace.

In Pakistan, management is typically hierarchical, with a clear chain of command and emphasis on authority and respect for elders. Decision-making is often centralized, with top-level managers making key decisions.

Sri Lankan management style is influenced by the country's Buddhist and Hindu values, which emphasize harmony and balance. Decision-making is often based on consensus, and there is a strong emphasis on building personal relationships and maintaining harmony in the workplace.

In Afghanistan, management style is heavily influenced by the country's tribal and Islamic traditions. There is a strong emphasis on respect for authority and hierarchy, and decision-making often involves consultation with elders or tribal leaders.

African Management Styles: Colonialism and Tribalism

In Africa, colonialism and tribalism have influenced management styles. Managers may be expected to be authoritative and directive, with decision-making centralized in senior management. Respect for authority and loyalty to the organization are highly valued, and performance is often measured in terms of

job security and loyalty to the organization. Personal relationships and tribal connections are also essential, and business negotiations may involve building trust and rapport over time.

Latin American Management Styles: Machismo and Collectivism

In Latin America, machismo and collectivism influence management styles. Managers may be expected to be strong, assertive, and charismatic, with decision-making centralized in senior management. Loyalty to the organization is highly valued, and personal relationships and networks are essential. In these cultures, performance is often measured in terms of loyalty to the organization and group achievement.

Implications for Global Business: Navigating Cultural Differences

Understanding and appreciating cultural differences is essential for success in global business. Managers must learn to navigate and respect cultural differences in order to effectively lead and manage teams across cultures. This may involve adapting management styles and communication styles to fit the cultural context, building trust and relationships, and developing cross-cultural competence.

Conclusion: The Importance of Understanding Cultural Influences on Management Styles

In today's global business environment, understanding and appreciating cultural influences on management styles is essential. Managers must be able to adapt their leadership and management styles to fit the cultural context in order to effectively lead and manage teams across cultures. By recognizing and respecting cultural differences, managers can build trust and relationships, facilitate communication, and ultimately drive success in global business.

Conclusion

As a manager's manager, your role is critical to the success of your team and your organization. Throughout this book, we have discussed key strategies and tactics for effective leadership, including building relationships with upper management, managing up, and building resilience and managing stress. In this final chapter, we will summarize the key takeaways from this book, reflect on the role of a manager's manager, and issue a call to action for readers to apply these strategies and tactics in their own leadership roles.

Summary of Key Takeaways

Throughout this book, we have emphasized the importance of building strong relationships with upper management, managing up effectively, and developing resilience and managing stress. We have also discussed the importance of setting clear goals and expectations, providing regular feedback and coaching, and dealing with underperformers and difficult conversations. Other key takeaways include the importance of effective communication, navigating office politics and power dynamics, and prioritizing self-care and work-life balance.

Reflection on the Role of a Manager's Manager

As a manager's manager, you play a critical role in supporting and developing your team. You are responsible for building relationships with upper management, managing up effectively, and navigating the complex dynamics of the workplace. You must also lead by example and model the behaviors and attitudes that you expect from your team. This requires a combination of leadership skills, emotional intelligence, and strategic thinking.

Call to Action for Readers

As a reader of this book, you have a unique opportunity to apply these strategies and tactics in your own leadership role. Whether you are a new manager's manager or an experienced leader, you can benefit from the insights and best practices shared in this book. We encourage you to reflect on your own leadership style and identify areas where you can improve. We also encourage you to experiment with new approaches and seek feedback from your team and colleagues. By applying these strategies and tactics, you can become a more effective and successful manager's manager.

In conclusion, the role of a manager's manager is complex and challenging, but also rewarding and fulfilling. By building strong relationships with upper management, managing up effectively, and developing resilience and managing stress, you can support and develop your team and achieve your organizational goals. We hope that this book has provided you with valuable insights and best practices for effective leadership, and we encourage you to apply these strategies and tactics in your own leadership role.

Inspirational Quotes on Management

"Management is about persuading people to do things they do not want to do, while leadership is about inspiring people to do things they never thought they could." — Steve Jobs

≈

"Good management consists in showing average people how to do the work of superior people." — John D. Rockefeller

≈

"Forget about the fast lane. If you really want to fly, just harness your power to your passion." — Oprah Winfrey

≈

"Leadership is the art of giving people a platform for spreading ideas that work." — Seth Godin

≈

"The first rule of management is delegation. Don't try and do everything yourself because you can't." — Anthea Turner

≈

"Good business leaders create a vision, articulate the vision, passionately own the vision and relentlessly drive it to completion." — Jack Welch

≈

"You are where you are today because you stand on somebody's shoulders. And wherever you are heading, you cannot get

there by yourself. If you stand on the shoulders of others, you have a reciprocal responsibility to live your life so that others may stand on your shoulders. It's the quid pro quo of life. We exist temporarily through what we take, but we live forever through what we give." — Vernon Jordan

≈

"Good management is the art of making problems so interesting and their solutions so constructive that everyone wants to get to work and deal with them." — Paul Hawken

≈

"Leadership and learning are indispensable to each other." — John F. Kennedy

≈

"If your actions inspire others to dream more, learn more, do more and become more, you are a leader." — John Quincy Adams

≈

"Real leaders are ordinary people with extraordinary determinations." — John Seaman Garns

≈

"Leaders are made, they are not born. They are made by hard effort." — Vince Lombardi

≈

"A real leader faces the music even when he doesn't like the tune." — Arnold H. Glasgow

≈

"Treat employees like they make a difference and they will." — Jim Goodnight

≈

"The challenge of leadership is to be strong, but not rude; be kind, but not weak; be bold, but not bully; be thoughtful, but not lazy; be humble, but not timid; be proud, but not arrogant; have humor, but without folly." — Jim Rohn

≈

"Corporate culture matters. How management chooses to treat its people impacts everything—for better or for worse." — Simon Sinek

≈

"Management is the opportunity to help people become better people. Practiced that way, it's a magnificent profession" — Clayton Christenson

≈

"Management's job is to convey leadership's message in a compelling and inspiring way. Not just in meetings, but also by example." — Jeffrey Gitomer

≈

"An employee's motivation is a direct result of the sum of interactions with his or her manager." — Bob Nelson

≈

"A leader takes people where they want to go. A great leader takes people where they don't necessarily want to go, but ought to be." — Rosalynn Carter

≈

"Leadership is the art of getting someone else to do something you want done because he wants to do it." — Dwight D. Eisenhower

≈

"Start with the end in mind." — Stephen Covey

≈

"The ability to learn is the most important quality a leader can have." — Padmasree Warrior

≈

"People respond well to those that are sure of what they want." — Anna Wintour

≈

"You need to be aware of what others are doing, applaud their efforts, acknowledge their successes and encourage them in their pursuits. When we all help one another, everybody wins." — Jim Stovall

≈

"The way management treats associates is exactly how the associates will treat the customers." — Sam Walton

≈

"The art of effective listening is essential to clear communication and clear communication is necessary to management success." — James Cash Penney

≈

REFERENCES:

Books:

"The Effective Manager" by Mark Horstman

"Crucial Conversations: Tools for Talking When Stakes Are High" by Kerry Patterson, Joseph Grenny, Ron McMillan, and Al Switzler

"The First 90 Days: Proven Strategies for Getting Up to Speed Faster and Smarter" by Michael Watkins

"Radical Candor: Be a Kick-Ass Boss Without Losing Your Humanity" by Kim Scott

"The 5 Languages of Appreciation in the Workplace" by Gary Chapman and Paul White

Articles:

"Managing Up: A Critical Skill for Effective Leadership" by John Baldoni (Harvard Business Review)

"5 Ways to Manage Up Effectively" by Dana Brownlee (Forbes)

"The Importance of Managing Up and How to Do It Effectively" by Deborah Sweeney (Entrepreneur)

"Stress Management for Managers: Tips and Tricks for Success" by Emily Bonnie (The Balance Careers)

"5 Habits of Resilient Managers" by Sabina Nawaz (Harvard Business Review)

These resources can provide additional insights and guidance for managers looking to improve their leadership skills and effectiveness.

About David Alan Binder

EDUCATION

BS Mount Mercy College with honors on the Dean's List

MPA, San Diego State University 3.4 gpa

Alliant Energy Graduate of the 5 year Manager's Training Course

PROFESSIONAL EXPERIENCE

Half a century as *Author and Writer*

18 years as a *Manager (Senior)*

13 years as a *Supervisor*

5 years in *Engineering*

7 years as a *Equipment Designer / Draftsman*

ADDITIONAL EXPERIENCE

Award Winning Author

Books written:

Effects of Environmental Pollution on Properties

The Manager's Manager: Strategies and Tactics for Effective Leadership

Exploring Phycology or Algology: A Comprehensive Guide to Algae and their Significance

A Chapter Book

8 Children's Picture Books

An Anthology of Poetry 1971 to Present

Procedures Writer, Author of Instruction Manuals, Author of How To Booklets

Teacher, Instructor, Trainer

Speaker at professional association conferences

Leadership, teaching, training, mentoring elementary to college

Connect with D. A. Binder at https://www.davidalanbinder.com or via FaceBook

